CGP makes Year 2 English simple!

This brilliant CGP book explains everything pupils will learn in Year 2 English — it's packed with clear, friendly notes and examples for every topic.

There are plenty of helpful practice questions throughout the book, plus progress tests at the start and end. All the answers are included at the back, so it's easy to check how pupils are getting on.

And of course, everything's matched to the latest KS1 National Curriculum. It's the perfect companion for the whole year!

What CGP is all about

Our sole aim here at CGP is to produce the highest quality books — carefully written, immaculately presented and dangerously close to being funny.

Then we work our socks off to get them out to you — at the cheapest possible prices.

Contents

About This Book 1
Start of Year Two Test 2

Section One — Grammar

Nouns and Noun Phrases 6
Verbs 8
Adjectives 10
Adverbs 12
Types of Sentences 14
Tenses 16
Joining Words 18

Section Two — Punctuation

Capital Letters 20
Ending Sentences 22
Commas 24
Apostrophes 26

Section Three — Vocabulary

Suffixes — Plurals 28
Suffixes — Other Endings 30
Compound Words 32

Section Four — Spelling

Vowel Sounds 34
The Soft 'c' and Hard 'c' Sounds 38
The Soft 'g' Sound 40
Silent 'k', 'g' and 'w' 42
Words Ending in 'le', 'el', 'al' and 'il' 44
The 'zh' Sound and Words Ending in 'tion' 46
Adding 'ing', 'ed', 'er', 'est' and 'y' to Words 48
Homophones and Other Words 52

Section Five — Reading Carefully

Finding Information — Stories 54
Finding Information — Non-fiction 56
Explaining Why 58
Putting Things in Order 60
Thinking About Words 62

Section Six — Thinking About the Text

Making Assumptions 64
What Happens Next? 66

Section Seven — Types of Text

Stories 68
Information Texts 70
Poems 72

Year Two Objectives Test 74
Glossary 78
Answers 80

Published by CGP

Editors:
Claire Boulter, Eleanor Claringbold, Kelsey Hammond, Katharine Howell,
Hannah Roscoe and Matt Topping.

With thanks to James Summersgill and Lucy Towle for the proofreading.
With thanks to Emily Smith for the copyright research.

ISBN: 978 1 78908 420 7

Printed by Elanders Ltd, Newcastle upon Tyne.
Clipart from Corel®
Thumb illustration used throughout the book © iStock.com

Based on the classic CGP style created by Richard Parsons.

Text, design, layout and original illustrations © Coordination Group Publications Ltd. (CGP) 2019
All rights reserved.

Photocopying more than one section of this book is not permitted, even if you have a CLA licence.
Extra copies are available from CGP with next day delivery • 0800 1712 712 • www.cgpbooks.co.uk

About This Book

This Book has All the Topics for Year 2

By the end of Year 2, you should be comfortable with all the English topics in this book.

There are two pages on most topics.

- The first page shows you what you need to know.
- The second page has questions to see what you can do.

> This book covers all the Year 2 content from the Key Stage 1 English Programme of Study.

This book also has two practice tests. The one at the front of the book tests what you know at the start of Year 2. The one at the back is to see what you've learnt by the end of the year.

Each Topic has a Question Page

These questions are colour-coded to show how difficult they are.

> Answers are at the back of the book.

 1 Easier   2 A bit harder   3 Challenging

There are Learning Objectives for Each Topic

Learning objectives say what you should be able to do.

Use the tick circles to show how happy you feel with each topic.

> You can use the tick circles for ongoing assessment to record which learning objectives have been met.

Tick here if you feel happy with the whole topic.

Tick here if you need a bit more practice.

Tick here if you're finding it really tricky.

"I can use commas in lists."

Start of Year Two Test

1) Circle the words that need a **capital letter**.

amy   donkey   tuesday

you   july   party

1 mark

2) Draw lines to match the words that **rhyme**.

boot   fern   snail

burn   flute   pale

1 mark

3) Rearrange all the letters in the box to make a word ending in 'nk'. The first letter of the word is in **bold**.

| n | a | **t** | k | h |

_____

1 mark

4) Draw a line to match each sentence to the correct **punctuation mark**.

What is your name   ?

What fun this is   .

I like strawberries   !

1 mark

5 Write the sentence below using **spaces**. Use the picture to help you.

Steveplaystheguitar.

_____

1 mark

6 Choose a **consonant** from the box to complete each word below.

| w   t   r   f |

c____ab   ____ly   s____im   ____rain

1 mark

7 Put a **tick** next to the sentences that **make sense**.

The cow eats the grass. ☐

Cousin my Wales in lives. ☐

Rumi is my best friend. ☐

1 mark

8 The words below are spelt wrong. Rewrite them **correctly** on the lines.

beerd   toylet   niet

_____   _____   _____

1 mark

Start of Year Two Test

9 Tick the sentence that describes each picture.

Katya is playing basketball. ☐
Katya is drawing a picture. ☐

Ekrem throws the ball. ☐
Ekrem swings his bat. ☐

Dan and Jo are sledging. ☐
Dan and Jo are skating. ☐

☐ 1 mark

Read the story and answer the questions below.

Rory's gran was ill. Rory went to see her. He took her a card to cheer her up. The card had yellow flowers on it. Gran smiled when she saw Rory.

10 **What** did Rory give to his gran?

_____

☐ 1 mark

11 How do you think Rory's gran **felt** when he visited her?

upset ☐   annoyed ☐   happy ☐

☐ 1 mark

Start of Year Two Test

Read the story and answer the questions below.

> Kartik the dragon was having a birthday party. There were balloons, party hats and a huge chocolate cake.
>
> At three o'clock, Kartik's friends started to arrive.
>
> Kartik got lots of presents. Ada the unicorn gave him some fairy dust. Sita the sea monster gave him a magic starfish. The best present was from Tommy the troll. He gave Kartik some of his special green slime.

12 What **didn't** Kartik have at the party?

    balloons ☐   cake ☐   a bouncy castle ☐

1 mark

13 **When** did Kartik's friends arrive?

_____

1 mark

14 Which present was Kartik's **favourite**?

    Ada's present   Sita's present   Tommy's present
    ☐   ☐   ☐

1 mark

15 How do you know it was his favourite?

_____

1 mark

Start of Year Two Test

Nouns and Noun Phrases

Nouns are words that name things

flower   Paris   Rosie

Noun phrases have nouns and other words

You can add words to a noun to describe it or to point out which noun you're talking about. This is called a noun phrase.

the fat cat

The writer is describing the cat.

this chair

The writer is pointing out which chair they're talking about.

Nouns and Noun Phrases

1 Add the **nouns** from the boxes to complete the sentences.

Eric   Spain   ball

I dropped the _____.

_____ is my best friend.

We are going to _____.

2 Circle the **noun** in each sentence.

My bike is yellow and blue.

The fireworks were very colourful.

The chickens ran around.

3 Tick the phrases that are **noun phrases**.

the red door ☐   a giant shoe ☐

that book ☐   very exciting ☐

later on ☐   talks slowly ☐

"I can identify and use nouns and noun phrases."

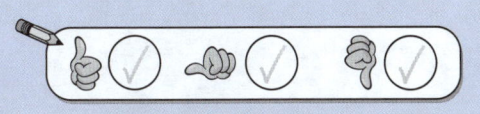

Section One — Grammar

Verts

Verbs are doing and being words

 The penguin <u>runs</u>.    The boots <u>are</u> blue.

The verb needs to <u>match</u> the <u>person</u> doing the <u>action</u>.

 I <u>read</u>.

She <u>reads</u>.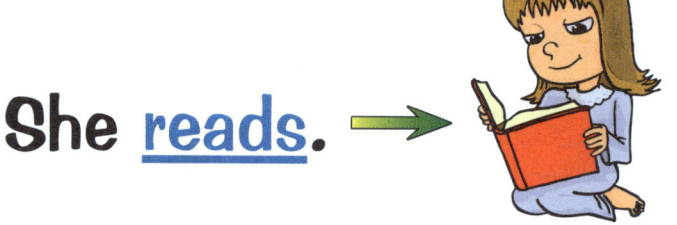

Verbs can have 'ing' on the end

Verbs with '<u>ing</u>' on the <u>end</u> show that something <u>is happening</u> or <u>was happening</u>.

 The chef is <u>cooking</u>.

The frog was <u>eating</u>.

Verbs

1 Tick the words that are **verbs**.

sing ☐   speak ☐

friendly ☐   tree ☐

music ☐   begin ☐

2 Circle the correct **verb** to complete each sentence.

Esmee (walk / walks) her pet dog.

My sister and I (love / loves) watching TV.

The cat (sleep / sleeps) by the fire.

3 Complete the **table** below by adding '**ing**' to the verbs.

Verb	Verb + 'ing'
float	floating
laugh	
roll	
stamp	

"I can identify and use verbs, including verbs with 'ing'."

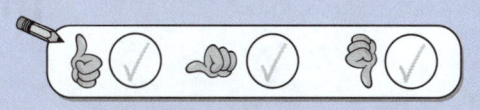

Adjectives

Adjectives are words that describe nouns

the green plant

a huge cake

an angry elephant

the evil witches

Adjectives can be used to compare things

This carrot is bigger than the other carrots.

This is the muddiest carrot.

This is the smallest carrot.

Adjectives

1 Add the correct **adjectives** to complete the sentences.

busy   melted   cheeky

I saw a _____ monkey at the zoo.

There is _____ chocolate on the sofa!

The bees were _____ making honey.

2 Circle the phrases that contain **adjectives**.

the fancy hat   they hid quickly   the book was old

cakes and pies   the hot weather   she yawned again

3 Add either '**er**' or '**est**' to the adjectives in the sentences below.

My sister is tall_____ than me.

I can jump the high_____ in my class.

Arlo's bedroom is clean_____ than Erin's.

"I can identify and use adjectives."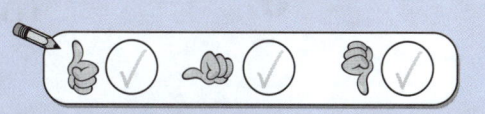

Section One — Grammar

Adverbs

Adverbs describe verbs

Adverbs tell you how the action was done.

The ship sailed smoothly.

It rained lightly.

Adverbs often end in 'ly'

Lots of adverbs are made by adding 'ly' to the end of an adjective.

strong → strongly

calm → calmly

If the word already ends in 'y', change the 'y' to an 'i', then add 'ly'.

messy → messily

funny → funnily

Section One — Grammar

Adverbs

1 Put a tick by the sentences that contain **adverbs**.

Yuri speaks politely. ☐

Liam gave her a new hat. ☐

I baked Anya some treats. ☐

Kat correctly guessed the answer. ☐

2 Circle the **correct** spelling to complete each sentence.

He (carefulily / carefully) poured the water.

The music was playing (noisily / noisyly).

3 Change the adjectives into **adverbs**.

adjective	adverb
mad	
fair	
sleepy	
healthy	

"I can identify and use adverbs."

Section One — Grammar

Types of Sentences

There are four different types of sentences

Words can be grouped together to form sentences.
Sentences can be statements, commands, questions or exclamations.

Statements tell you something.

Commands give orders.

Questions ask something.

Exclamations show strong feelings.
They start with 'what' or 'how'.

Types of Sentences

1 Draw lines to match the sentences to the correct **label**.

The lemon is sour.   Where is the bus?

question

How old are you?   What time is it?

statement

Kelly plays football.   I lost my shoe.

2 Tick the sentences that are **exclamations**.

What a hard race that was! ☐

Dinner will be ready soon. ☐

Where is your pencil case? ☐

How nice to see you again! ☐

3 Circle the correct **label** to describe each sentence.

Put that book away.   ⟶   (command / question)

Why did you do that?   ⟶   (question / statement)

How lovely that was!   ⟶   (command / exclamation)

Bananas are yellow.   ⟶   (exclamation / statement)

"I can identify different sentence types."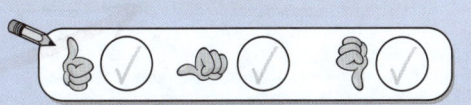

Section One — Grammar

Tenses

Tenses tell you when something happens

You can use the simple present to talk about now.

She floats. The captain looks.

You can use the simple past to talk about something that's finished.

The elephant painted. He cleaned.

Stick to one tense in sentences

The verbs in a sentence are usually in the same tense.

I play the piano and I sing.

Both of these verbs are in the present tense.

She tripped and bruised her knee.

Both of these verbs are in the past tense.

Section One — Grammar

Tenses

1 Circle the phrases which use the **simple past** tense.

we landed   they joke   Priya jumped

Finn swims   I finished   she bakes

2 Complete the table by writing the phrases in the **simple present** tense and **simple past** tense.

simple present	simple past
I live	
	Zoe packed
Ben washes	

3 Circle the verb in the correct **tense** to complete each sentence.

Sam (used / uses) glasses when she reads.

Mum watched as I (stir / stirred) the soup.

She (asks / asked) before she played outside.

"I can identify different tenses and stick to one when I use sentences."

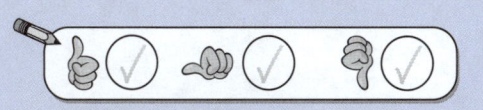

Joining Words

'When', 'if', 'that' and 'because' join sentences

You can use the words 'when', 'if', 'that' and 'because' to join sentences together.

He wears a crown because he is the king.

The mouse comes out when the cat is sleeping.

'And', 'but' and 'or' also join sentences

You can also use 'and', 'but' and 'or' to join sentences together.

It is a monkey and it is wearing a bow.

We have strawberry ice cream or we have vanilla ice cream.

Joining Words

1 Circle the **joining word** in each sentence.

We can have lunch if you are hungry.

Lucy saw Libby when she was shopping.

Jamal wore a hat that his mum knitted.

2 Circle the correct **joining word** to complete each sentence.

I got in trouble (because / if) of my sister.

Simon liked the picture (when / that) I drew.

They went to bed, (but / or) they weren't tired.

Dad cooked dinner (or / and) it was tasty.

3 Complete each sentence using the **joining words** in the boxes. Use each joining word **once**.

I got new shoes, ___but___ they were too small.

His sister is five _____ his brother is six.

Put your coat on _____ you will get cold.

| and |
| or |
| ~~but~~ |

"I can join sentences together using joining words."

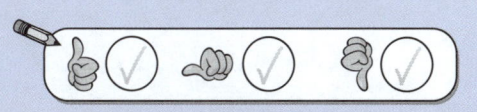

Section One — Grammar

Capital Letters

Start every sentence with a capital letter

My socks are green.

Thank you for the tea.

Lions like to sleep.

Use capital letters for names and 'I'

Use capital letters for the names of people and places.
Also use capital letters for the days of the week and for 'I'.

Ryan has two pet rabbits.

We are going to London.

The party is on Friday.

When I was six, I had a dog.

Capital Letters

1 Read the sentences below. Write the **name** of the person who uses **capital letters** correctly.

Kim — there are Birds in the park.

Eli — There are birds in the park.

_____ uses capital letters correctly.

2 Draw lines to match the words with the correct **label**.

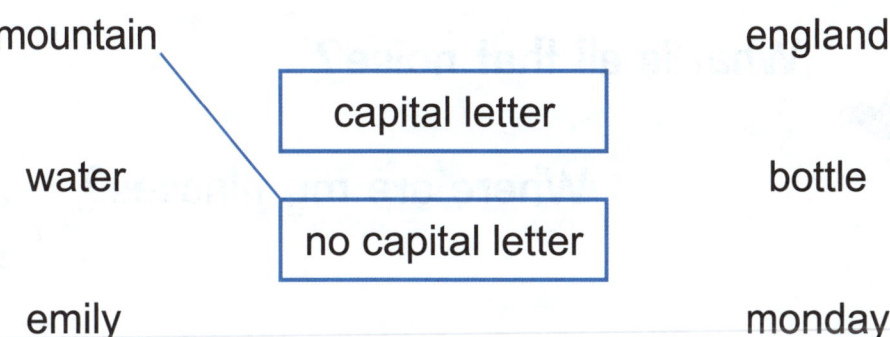

mountain — capital letter — england

water — no capital letter — bottle

emily — monday

3 Rewrite each sentence with **capital letters** in the correct places.

next week, i am going to france.

_____

let's visit mike on sunday.

_____

"I can use capital letters at the start of sentences and for names and 'I'."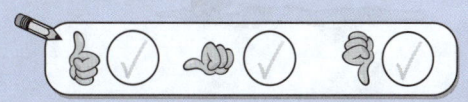

Section Two — Punctuation

Ending Sentences

Sentences usually end with a full stop

I am going home soon.

She is having a bath.

Every question ends with a question mark

What is all that noise?

Where are my glasses?

Some sentences end with exclamation marks

Sentences that show strong feelings or someone speaking loudly should end with an exclamation mark.

How awful this weather is!

What a friendly cat you are!

He's got our sausages!

Section Two — Punctuation

Ending Sentences

1 Read the text below. Put a tick in the boxes where there should be a **full stop**.

I am going to the shop ☐   Do you want anything ☐

I'll be back soon ☐   Where are my keys ☐

2 Tick the sentences which use **question marks** correctly.

I want to watch TV? ☐

Can you get me a drink? ☐

What a long dog that is? ☐

Is this your hat? ☐

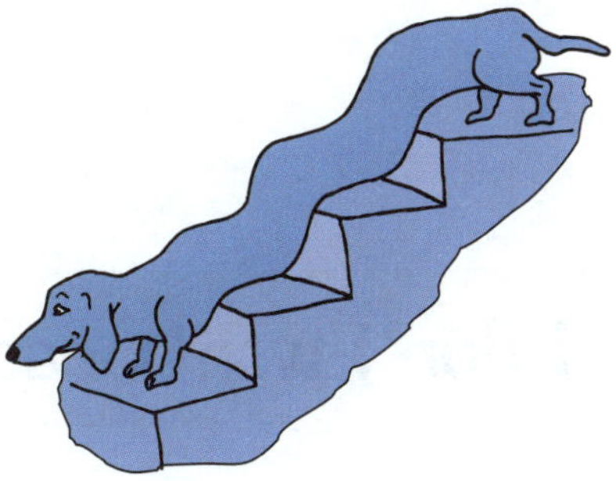

3 Rewrite the sentence in the correct order with the correct **punctuation**.

| hill | ~~a~~ | big | ~~What~~ | that | is |

What a _____

"I can use full stops, question marks and exclamation marks."

Section Two — Punctuation

Commas

Commas are used to separate things in a list

You need a comma between all the things in a list except the last two. Write 'and' or 'or' between the last two things.

I like to swim, paint and cook.

I don't want peas, carrots or beans.

He knitted a hat, a scarf, some mittens and a jumper.

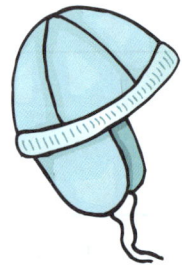  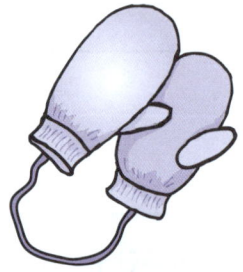 

Commas

1 Tick the sentences that use **commas** correctly.

The water was deep, dark and cold. ☐

We can bake biscuits cake, or bread. ☐

I saw fish, crabs and a shark. ☐

The kittens are small, fluffy, and cute. ☐

2 Add a **comma** to each of the lists below.

Lara is scared of spiders wasps and lions.

My brothers are called Ed Ted and Ned.

You can play football hockey or cricket.

3 Rewrite the lists below with **commas**.

I drink juice water and milk.

_____

Violet doesn't like maths art or music.

_____

"I can use commas in lists."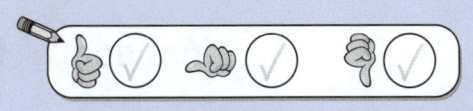

Section Two — Punctuation

Apostrophes

Apostrophes can replace *missing letters*

Sometimes, when two words are joined together, an apostrophe replaces a missing letter or letters.

I + am → I'm — The apostrophe replaces the 'a'.

they + are → they're

she + had → she'd — The apostrophe replaces the 'h' and the 'a'.

Apostrophes can tell you *who owns something*

An apostrophe and 's' on the end of a word shows that something belongs to someone.

the farmer's chicken

Lisa's bear

Jake's bike

the rhino's horn

You add 's' to the end of the owner's name.

Section Two — Punctuation

Apostrophes

1 Add apostrophes to the words in **bold**.

I **havent** got a coat.

I know **hes** hiding somewhere.

They **wont** eat cabbage.

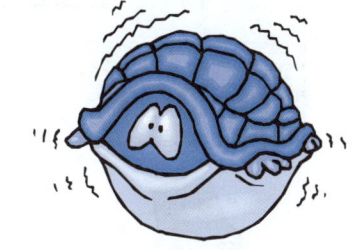

2 Complete the sentences with the **shortened** forms of the words in the boxes.

| has not | can not | she is |

I like my teacher because _____ kind.

My dad _____ find his tie.

The sun _____ come out yet.

3 Complete the sentences using the words in **bold** and an **apostrophe** and '**s**'.

The book belongs to **Kit**. ➡ It's ____Kit's____ book.

The puppy belongs to **Raj**. ➡ It's _____ puppy.

The pen belongs to **Liz**. ➡ It's _____ pen.

"I can use apostrophes for missing letters and to show possession."

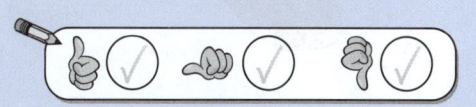

Suffixes — Plurals

Suffixes are letters added to the end of words

To make most singular words plural, add 's'.

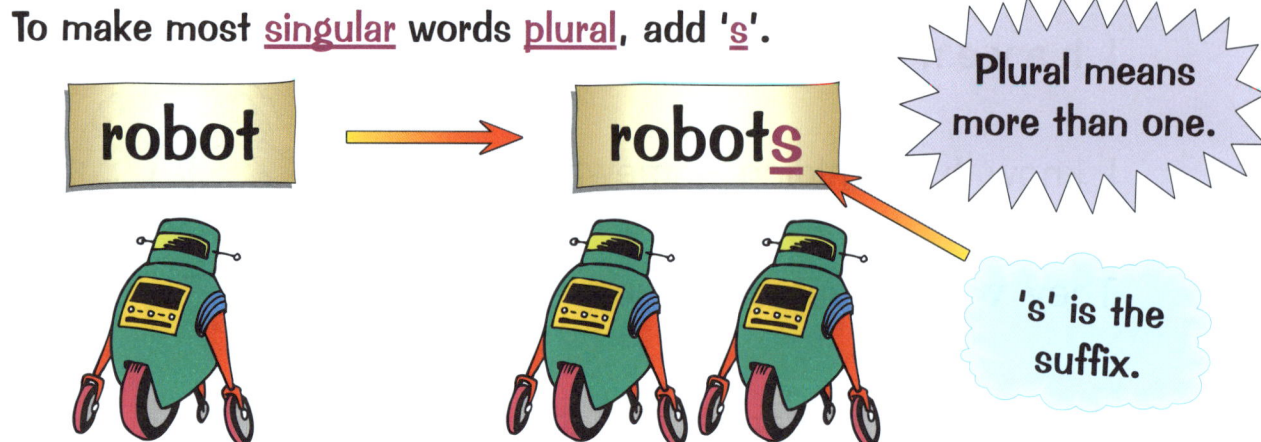

Plural means more than one.

's' is the suffix.

Add 'es' if the word ends in 'o', 's', 'x', 'z', 'ch' or 'sh'.

'es' is the suffix.

For words ending in a consonant and then 'y', you remove the 'y' and add 'ies'.

'ies' is the suffix.

Suffixes — Plurals

1 Add 's' or 'es' to the words below to make them **plural**.

house____   gas____

lion____   beach____

sash____   nose____

2 Write the **plural** of each word on the lines below.

story   *stories*   valley _____

penny _____   holiday _____

body _____   family _____

3 Put a **tick** by the sentences that use **suffixes** correctly.

The bird hid in the **branchs**. ☐

My **sisteres** are always singing. ☐

I want to travel to other **countries**. ☐

I have two **bunches** of bananas. ☐

"I can use suffixes to make words plural."

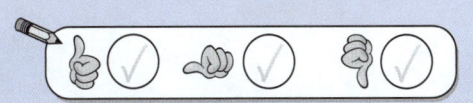

Section Three — Vocabulary

Suffixes — Other Endings

Add 'ment' or 'ness' to words to make nouns

move + ment = movement

↑ root word ↓

quiet + ness = quietness

Most of the time, you don't have to change the spelling of the root word — you just add the suffix onto the end.

Add 'ful' or 'less' to words to make adjectives

pain + ful = painful

noun — suffix — adjective

help + less = helpless

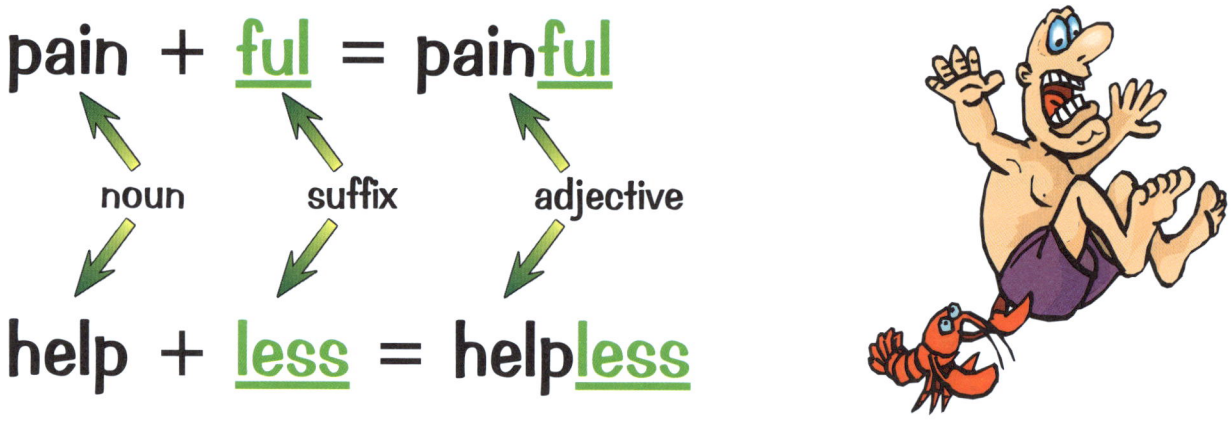

Tick all the suffixes which can be added to the word 'fear'.

ment ☐   ness ☐   ful ✓   less ✓

← 'fearful' and 'fearless' are both adjectives.

Section Three — Vocabulary

Suffixes — Other Endings

1 **Shade in** the suffixes that can be added to the word '**pain**'.

| less | ness | ment | ful |

2 Add '**ment**', '**ness**', '**ful**' or '**less**' to the words in bold. Use each suffix **once**.

The monkey is very **cheer**_____.

I was shocked at his **rude**_____.

Their **punish**_____ was fair.

Indu was totally **speech**_____.

3 **Tick** the sentences where the **correct** suffix has been added to the word in **bold**. For the words with incorrect suffixes, write the **correct suffix** on the line.

She stared at me in **amazeless**. ☐   ment

Please make yourself **useness**. ☐   _____

I couldn't see in the **darkment**. ☐   _____

He was always very **careful**. ☐   _____

"I can use suffixes to make nouns and adjectives."

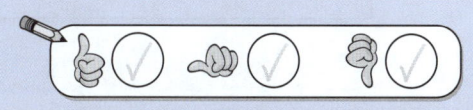

Section Three — Vocabulary

Compound Words

Join words to make a compound word

Two words can be joined together to make a compound word.

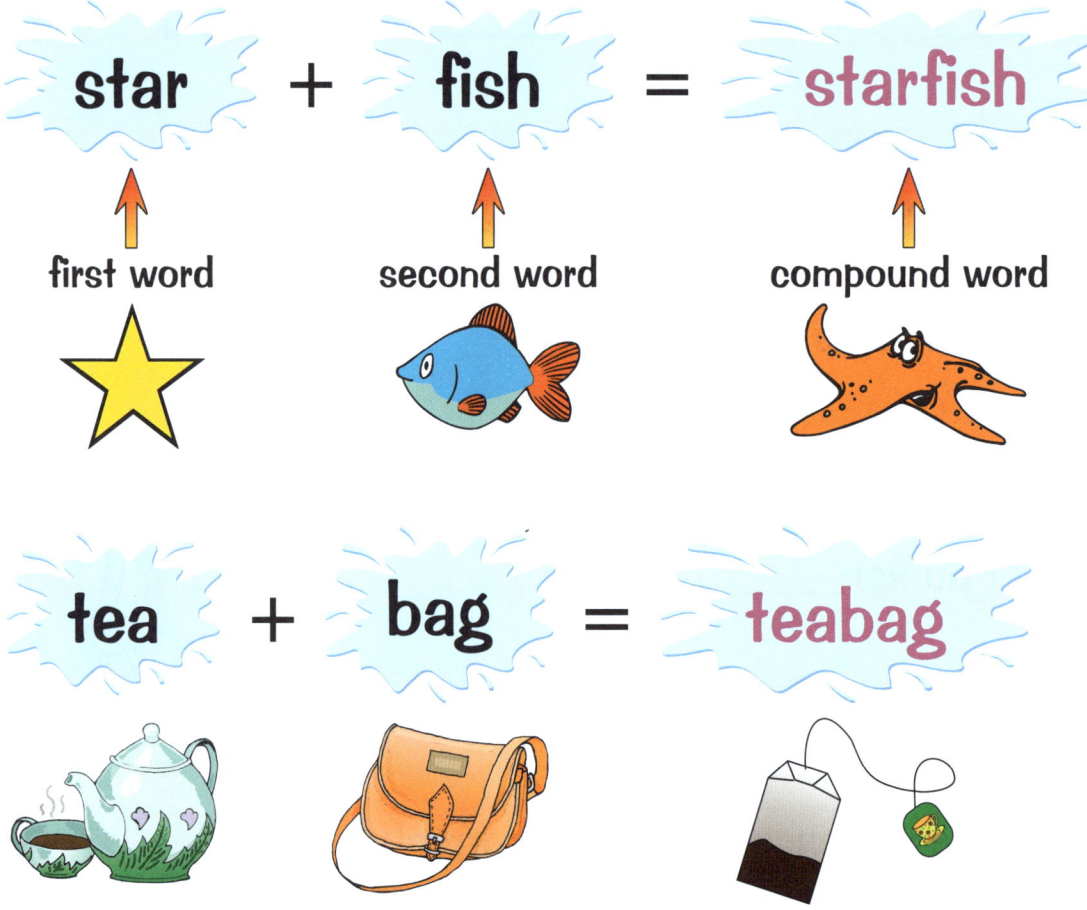

Circle the compound word in each sentence.

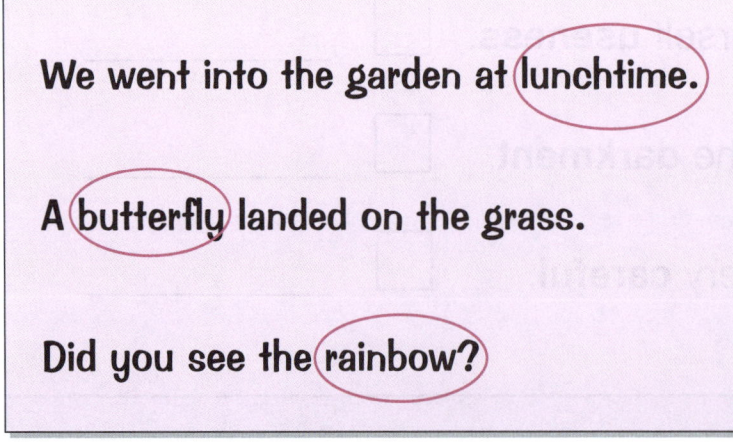

We went into the garden at (lunchtime.)

A (butterfly) landed on the grass.

Did you see the (rainbow?)

Section Three — Vocabulary

Compound Words

1 Circle the **compound word** in each sentence.

Maya couldn't find her hairbrush.

Remember to take your suitcase with you.

The bathroom is very cold.

2 Draw lines to join the words on the left to a word on the right to make a **compound word**.

shoe — brow

pan — lace

eye — cake

grand — son

3 Add a **noun** to each word to make **compound words**.

foot + _____ = _____

book + _____ = _____

snow + _____ = _____

"I can join words together to make compound words."

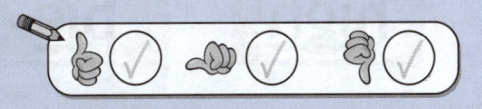

Section Three — Vocabulary

Vowel Sounds

The 'ai' sound

These words all contain the 'ai' sound, but it's spelt differently in each word.

rain   **cake**   **away**

At the end of words, an 'ai' sound is often written as 'ay'.

The long 'e' sound

The long 'e' sound can be spelt like this:

sheep   **beast**   **athlete**   **thief**

The short 'o' sound

This is the short 'o' sound:

spot   **wand**   **squat**

The short 'o' sound is usually written with an 'a' after 'w' and 'qu'.

The long 'i' sound

There are lots of different ways to spell the long 'i' sound.

high   **pie**   **kite**   **fly**

Vowel Sounds

1 Circle the word that is spelt **correctly** in each pair.

payn / pain   stray / strai   blame / blaim

plai / play   fayk / fake   stain / stayn

2 Fill in each gap with the correct **vowel sound** from the box.

| ea |
| ee |
| ie |

The mouse ate all of our ch____se.

The pr____st said a prayer.

The queen held a f____st.

3 Underline the **short 'o'** sound in each word.

wander   forgot   orange   swallow

4 Complete the **long 'i'** vowel sounds in these sentences.

The sk_____ looked dark and grey.

Sati is very pol____t____.

The butterfly has br_____t wings.

"I can spell the 'ai' sound, the long 'e' and 'i' sounds and the short 'o' sound."

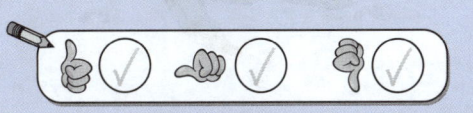

Section Four — Spelling

Vowel Sounds

The 'aw' sound

The 'aw' sound can be spelt in different ways:

str**aw**   t**al**k   aw**ar**d

The 'aw' sound is usually spelt 'ar' after 'w'.

The short 'u' sound

The short 'u' sound can be written with an 'o' or a 'u':

m**o**ther   **u**mbrella

c**o**ver   t**u**mble

The 'ur' sound

This is the 'ur' sound:

sh**ir**t   p**er**son   t**ur**tles   w**or**d

After a 'w', the 'ur' sound is spelt 'or'.

Section Four — Spelling

Vowel Sounds

1 Tick the words that are spelt **correctly**.

fawl ☐   yorn ☐   warm ☐

farll ☐   yawn ☐   wawm ☐

fall ☐   yaln ☐   walm ☐

2 Circle the words that are spelt **correctly** in these sentences.

We hid under the (covers / cuvers).

The (drommer / drummer) played us a beat.

The (munkey / monkey) swings in the trees.

3 Draw a line to match each word to its missing 'ur' sound.

w___ld   ur

c___ve   er

tw___l   or

p___son   ir

"I can spell the 'aw' sound, the short 'u' sound and the 'ur' sound."

Section Four — Spelling

The Soft 'c' and Hard 'c' Sounds

A soft 'c' sounds like an 's'

The soft 'c' sound can be written with an 's' or a 'c'.

 sock   sandal   serpent

Use 'c' before 'e', 'y' and 'i'.

 face   juicy   city

A hard 'c' sounds like a 'k'

The hard 'c' can be spelt with a 'k', a 'c' or 'ck'.

kitten   cousin   tru

Before 'e', 'i' and 'y', the hard 'c' sound is spelt with a 'k'.

'ck' often comes at the end of words.

Draw lines to show whether these words have a soft 'c' sound or a hard 'c' sound.

This is a hard 'c' sound because it sounds like 'k'.

This is a soft 'c' sound because it sounds like 's'.

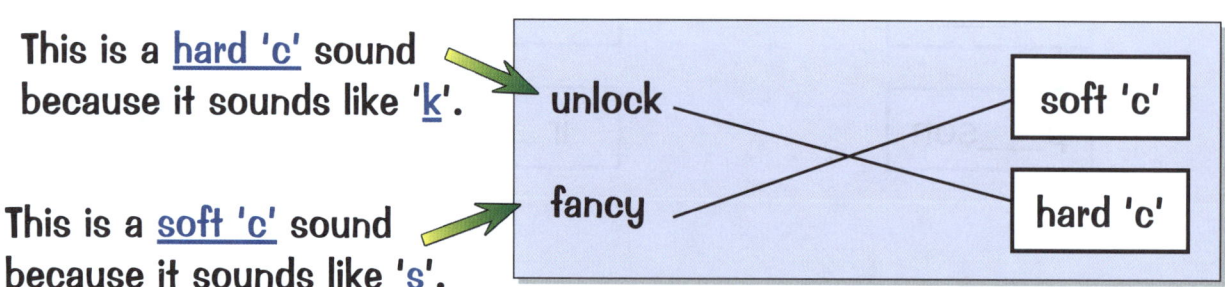

Section Four — Spelling

The Soft 'c' and Hard 'c' Sounds

1 Circle the words which are spelt **correctly**.

bisycle   ceed   salad   dancing

plase   sort   pensil   celebrate

2 Complete these sentences using the letters in the box.

| c | ck | k |

We need a map and a ____ompass.

Maria played a song on the ____eyboard.

The elephant was stu____.

3 Draw lines to show whether these words have a **soft** 'c' or a **hard** 'c' sound.

celery

carrot

surfer

octagon

hard 'c'

soft 'c'

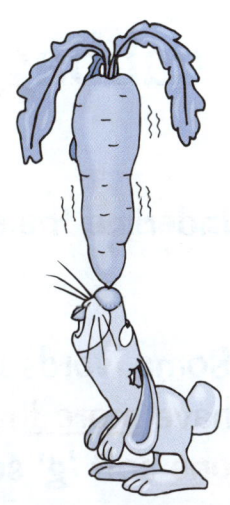

"I can spell the soft 'c' sound and the hard 'c' sound."

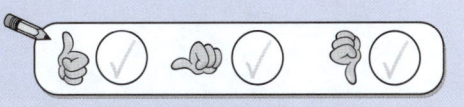

Section Four — Spelling

The Soft 'g' Sound

A soft 'g' sound sounds like a 'j'

The soft 'g' sound can be written with a 'j' or a 'g'.

j → jewels
joke
jumper

g → giraffe
magic
genius

At the end of words, use 'ge' or 'dge'

cabbage

hedge

Underline the soft 'g' sounds in the passage below.

Some words might have more than one soft 'g' sound.

The giant stomped out of the castle. Georgia hid under the bridge until he had gone. She had to escape urgently.

Section Four — Spelling

The Soft 'g' Sound

1 Circle the word which is spelt **correctly** in each pair.

ledge / lege   adge / age   imadge / image

fridge / frige   badge / bage   manadge / manage

2 Underline the **soft** 'g' sounds in the passage below.

The guide says we will need lots of energy, so we should take sugary snacks. I baked some ginger biscuits and angel cakes.

3 Complete these sentences with 'g', 'j', 'ge' or 'dge'.

Don't stand too close to the e_____.

The warrior had coura_____.

The car en_____ine is broken.

Marcus is good at _____uggling.

"I can spell the soft 'g' sound."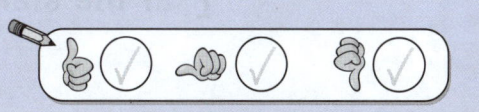

Silent 'k', 'g' and 'w'

You don't say silent letters

Silent letters are letters you don't say when you're reading a word aloud.

These are silent letters. → <u>k</u>nitting   <u>w</u>reck   <u>g</u>nash

'g' and 'k' are silent if they come before 'n'

These words would sound the same without the first letter:

<u>g</u>nome

<u>k</u>night

The letter 'w' is silent if it comes before 'r'

<u>w</u>riting

The letter '<u>w</u>' is silent before '<u>r</u>' at the start of words.

Section Four — Spelling

Silent 'k', 'g' and 'w'

1 Add a silent '**k**', '**g**' or '**w**' to these words.

__nife   __rap   __nat

__riggle   __nuckle   __narled

2 Write each word in the correct box.

gnarl   knee   wrestle   kangaroo   goat   knot   writer

silent 'k'	silent 'g'	silent 'w'	no silent letter

3 The words in bold have the wrong **silent letter**. Draw a line to match each sentence to the correct silent letter.

The dog **knawed** the bone.

k

We **gnocked** on the door.

g

Amir broke his **rrist**.

w

I **gnew** we had the wrong answer.

"I can spell words with a silent 'k', 'g' and 'w'."

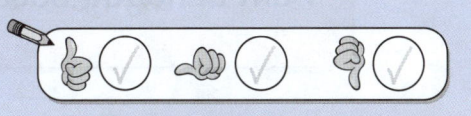

Section Four — Spelling

Words Ending in 'le', 'el', 'al' and 'il'

Some word endings sound the same

Some words sound like they have the same ending, but they don't. Make sure you learn how to spell words ending in 'le', 'el', 'al' and 'il'.

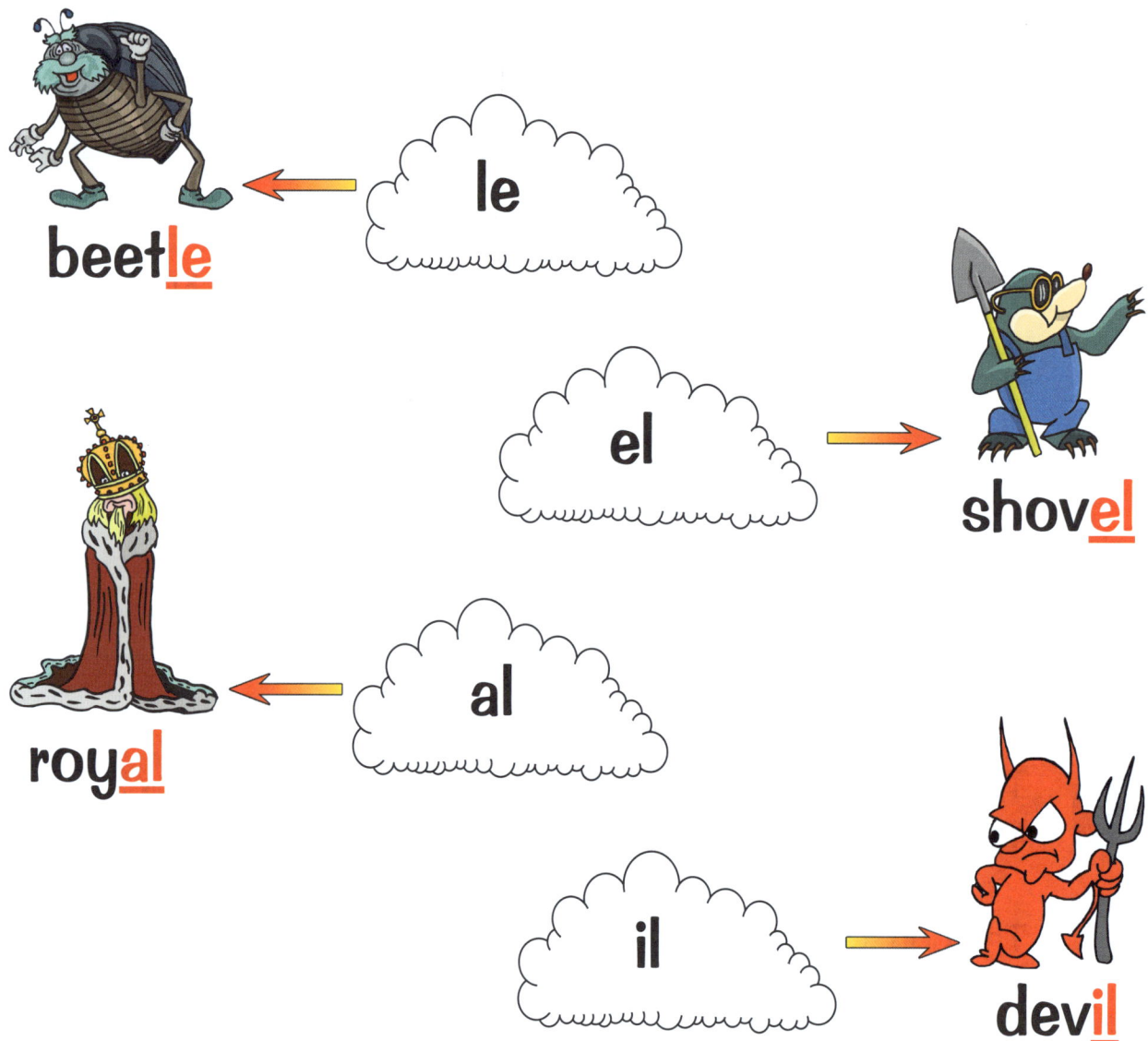

Complete these sentences with the correct word endings.

I saw a dinosaur foss**il** at the museum.

I am annoyed because my brother changed the chann**el**.

Words Ending in 'le', 'el', 'al' and 'il'

1 Tick the words that are spelt **correctly**.

pettle ☐   gerbel ☐   table ☐

petel ☐   gerbil ☐   tabal ☐

petal ☐   gerbal ☐   tabil ☐

2 Fill in each gap with the correct letters from the box.

| el |
| il |
| le |
| al |

In Apr_____, I am going to trav_____ to Wales with my family. We have to fit all of our things in our litt_____ car. While we are away, I want to try some loc_____ food.

3 Complete these sentences with the correct **word endings**.

There are scary creatures in the jung_____.

We dug a secret tunn_____ in our garden.

My favourite anim_____ is a sloth.

The witch cast an ev_____ spell.

"I can spell words that end in 'le', 'el', 'al' and 'il'."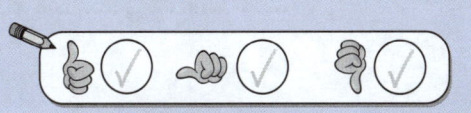

The 'zh' Sound and Words Ending in 'tion'

Some words have a 'zh' sound spelt 's'

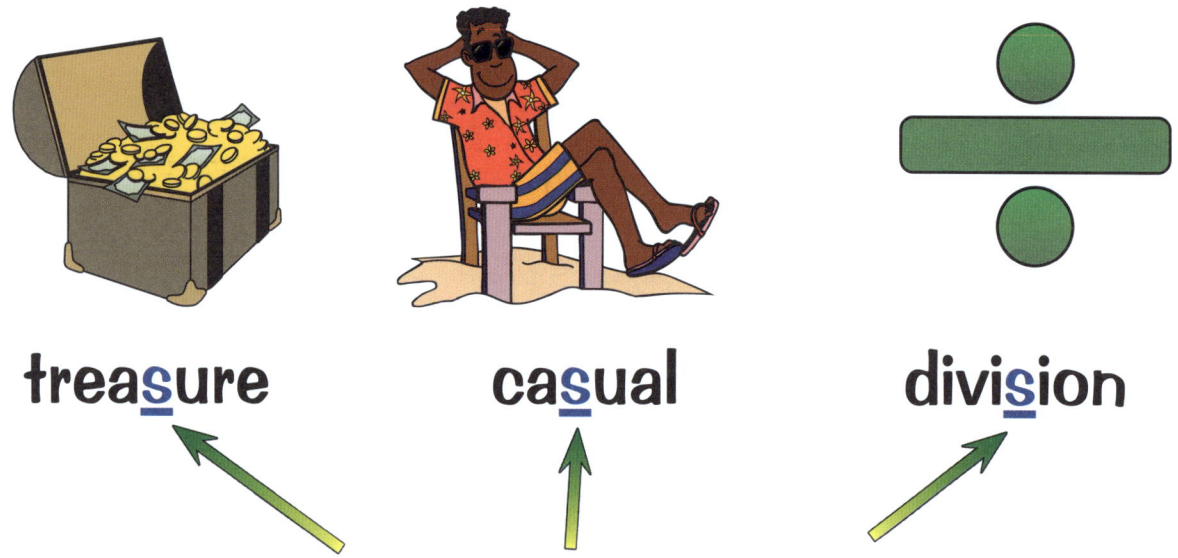

treasure   casual   division

The 's' in these words sounds like 'zh'.

Some words end in a 'shun' sound

The 'shun' sound is usually spelt 'tion'.

emotion   addition

The 'zh' Sound and Words Ending in 'tion'

1 Circle the words which have the 'zh' sound in them.

leisure   reason   decision

decisive   unusual   sure

2 Circle the **correct** spelling to complete each sentence.

There was an (explosion / explotion) in the lab.

Laura loves (acsion / action) films.

The (television / televition) was too loud.

The magic (posion / potion) turns you into a frog.

3 Draw lines to match each sentence to its missing **word ending**.

I wear glasses because my vi____ is poor.

Walk with cau____ on the ice.

In my confu____, I forgot my wallet.

I asked for a bigger por____.

sion

tion

"I can spell the 'zh' sound and words that end in 'tion'."

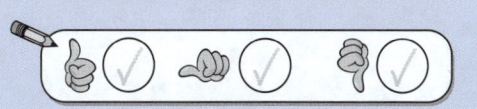

Adding 'ing', 'ed', 'er', 'est' & 'y' to Words

Suffixes change words ending in 'e'

When you add 'ing' or 'ed' to a word that ends in 'e', remove the final 'e' first.

smile + ing → smil**ing**
smile + ed → smil**ed**

You have to take away the 'e' at the end of 'smile' to add 'ing' and 'ed'.

Suffixes change some words ending in 'y'

When you add 'ing' or 'ed' to a word ending in a vowel and 'y', there is no spelling change.

play + ing → play**ing**
play + ed → play**ed**

When you add 'ing' to a word ending in a consonant and 'y', there is no spelling change.

cry + ing → cry**ing**

When you add 'ed' to a word ending in a consonant and 'y', change the 'y' to an 'i' first.

cry + ed → cr**ied**

Section Four — Spelling

Adding 'ing', 'ed', 'er', 'est' & 'y' to Words

1 Circle the **correct** spelling to complete each sentence.

Andrew (loved / loveed) travelling by train.

I'm (moveing / moving) house next month.

May (bakeed / baked) a cake, and she ate it all.

2 Fill in the **missing letter** in these words.

Rachel carr__ed the dog across the river.

I spent all day tid__ing my room.

Rob destro__ed his sandcastle.

The snails hurr__ed as fast as they could.

3 Complete the table by adding '**ing**' and '**ed**' to each word.

	ing	ed
live	living	lived
annoy		
fry		
dive		

"I can add 'ing' and 'ed' to words ending in 'e' and 'y'."

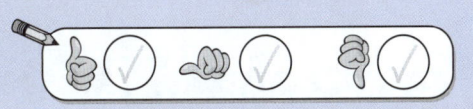

Adding 'ing', 'ed', 'er', 'est' & 'y' to Words

Sometimes you double the last letter

If you add '<u>ing</u>' or '<u>ed</u>' to a word ending with a <u>short vowel sound</u> and a <u>consonant</u>, you need to <u>double</u> the last letter.

Short vowel sounds are sounds like the '<u>a</u>' in '<u>bat</u>' or the '<u>o</u>' in '<u>cot</u>'.

'<u>er</u>' and '<u>est</u>' follow the rules for '<u>ing</u>' and '<u>ed</u>'

wise + est ➔ wis<u>est</u> — You have to <u>remove</u> the '<u>e</u>' from 'wise' before adding '<u>est</u>'.

shiny + er ➔ shin<u>ier</u> — The '<u>y</u>' in 'shiny' changes to '<u>i</u>' before adding '<u>er</u>'.

hot + er ➔ hot<u>ter</u> — The letter '<u>t</u>' in 'hot' is doubled when you add '<u>er</u>'.

Adding '<u>y</u>' follows the same rules as '<u>ed</u>'

risk + y   ease + y   chat + y
risk<u>y</u>   eas<u>y</u>   chat<u>ty</u>

Adding 'ing', 'ed', 'er', 'est' & 'y' to Words

1 Circle the words where the **last letter** needs to be **doubled** to add '**ed**'.

pop   help   chant

rob   drag   park

2 Complete these sentences by adding '**ing**'. You may need to **double** the **last letter**.

The rhino is nap_____ in the sun.

I am listen_____ to music.

Sobia is cut_____ the grass.

3 Complete the table by adding '**er**' and '**est**' to the words.

	er	est
long		
strange		
comfy		

4 Add the suffix '**y**' to these words.

hand ➡ _____   snap ➡ _____   ice ➡ _____

"I can double letters when adding suffixes, and I can add 'er', 'est' and 'y' to words."

Homophones and Other Words

Homophones are words that sound the same

Homophones are words that sound the same but have different meanings and spellings.

blew   blue   sail   sale

berry   bury   sun   son

Some words you just need to learn

Some words don't follow the rules.
You have to learn how to spell these words.

plant   door   money   cold

Homophones and Other Words

1 Circle the correct **homophone** to complete these sentences.

I can (here / hear) music coming from upstairs.

The (be / bee) is buzzing from flower to flower.

Alex is going (to / too) the cinema.

We are going in (there / their) car.

2 Fill in the **missing letters** in these words.

Mum won't let me clim____ the tree.

There is a pot of g____ld at the end of the rainbow.

We are two ____ours away from the airport.

I packed some cl____th____s for my holiday.

3 In each sentence, underline the word that is spelt **incorrectly**. Rewrite the words correctly on the lines.

There is a monster behined the sofa. _____

The artwork in the school is pritty. _____

The beach is very bisy today. _____

"I can spell homophones and common exception words."

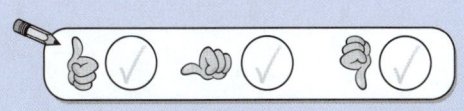

Section Four — Spelling

Section Five — Reading Carefully

54

Finding Information — Stories

You can answer questions by reading the story

To answer a question, you need to look at the writing.
The answer to the question will be in the story.

A Nature Walk

Alisha and Harrison were walking through the forest. It was a sunny day, but the trees were so thick that only a little bit of sunlight made it through the overhanging branches to light their way along the path. Suddenly, Harrison stopped walking and pointed at the ground.

"Look, there are some animal footprints," said Harrison.

"I don't know what kind of animal made them," said Alisha. "Let's follow them."

Where were Alisha and Harrison walking? Tick one box.

Alisha and Harrison were walking through the forest, so this is the right answer.

- the desert ☐   the park ☐
- the forest ✓   the beach ☐

Finding Information — Stories

Read the rest of the story and answer the questions.

> "It might not be safe," said Harrison. "What if we get lost?"
> "We won't get lost because I have a map and a compass," replied Alisha.
> They crept through the trees, following the tracks. As they came towards a clearing, they heard a rustling noise. Pushing through the branches, they saw a bear munching on berries. He stared at Alisha and Harrison and then plodded away.

1) What was Harrison worried about? Tick **one** box.

finding a bear ☐   getting lost in the forest ☐

not having enough food ☐   it getting dark ☐

2) What **two** things did Alisha have with her?

_____

_____

3) What did the bear do after he saw Alisha and Harrison?

_____

"I can find information in stories."

Section Five — Reading Carefully

Finding Information — Non-fiction

You need to read non-fiction writing carefully

The answer to a question might be in a piece of non-fiction writing. Just like a story, you need to read the writing carefully.

Titles tell you what the whole page is about.

Subheadings can help you find the information you need.

How to make Alien Feelers

What you need

- a headband
- two green pipe cleaners
- two green pom poms
- a pencil
- sticky tape
- glue

Method

- Wrap one end of each pipe cleaner around the headband. Use sticky tape to hold them in place.
- Use a pencil to make a small hole in each pom pom and put a small drop of glue inside each hole.
- Put the free end of each pipe cleaner into the hole in the pom pom. You are ready to wear your feelers!

What is the sticky tape used for?

Holding the pipe cleaners in place.

Section Five — Reading Carefully

Finding Information — Non-fiction

Read this piece of non-fiction writing and answer the questions.

> **Crested gecko lizards**
>
> **What to feed your gecko**
>
> You should feed a young gecko daily, but older geckos only need feeding every two days. They like to eat insects, especially crickets. If your gecko won't eat crickets, try giving it mealworms instead.
>
> **Where to keep your gecko**
>
> Geckos should be kept in a large tank. Use a heat lamp to heat one side of the tank, so your gecko has a warm area to relax in and a colder area to cool down.

1 Which of these are subheadings? Tick **two** boxes.

Crested gecko lizards ☐   What to feed your gecko ☐

They like to eat insects ☐   Where to keep your gecko ☐

2 How often should you feed an adult gecko?

_____

3 What should you use to heat the gecko's tank?

_____

"I can find information in non-fiction writing."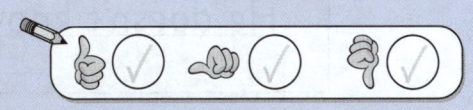

Section Five — Reading Carefully

Explaining Why

You might need to explain *why*

Sometimes you have to explain why something happens or why something has been included in a bit of writing.

Bubbles the Explorer

Bubbles the fish had spent his whole life on the same coral reef. He had <u>eaten the same seaweed and swum past the same seashells every day</u>. One day, as he <u>drifted dully</u> around the reef, he decided it was finally time to explore the ocean.

The next day, he packed a map and some food, and set off. <u>He had never been beyond the reef before</u>, and he was excited to see what the ocean had in store for him.

This shows that Bubbles is <u>bored</u> of doing and seeing the <u>same things</u> every day.

This shows that Bubbles hasn't been out into the ocean before, so he <u>won't know where he's going</u>.

Why does Bubbles decide to go exploring?

<u>He is bored of living on the reef.</u>

Why does Bubbles pack a map?

<u>He doesn't know his way around outside of the reef.</u>

Explaining Why

Read the piece of writing below and answer the questions.

> **Dog Lovers Wanted!**
> The 'Puppy Pad' kennel is looking for people to help look after our adorable dogs in July. With so many people going on holiday, we have more dogs than usual. We want people to take our dogs for walks, play with them and feed them. If you enjoy being outside and love dogs, please apply.

1 Why do you think the writer chose to include when they need people to work? Tick **one** box.

The writer only wants people who are free in July to apply. ☐

The writer is on holiday in July. ☐

The writer doesn't need any more staff in July. ☐

2 Why do you think the kennel needs more people in July?

_____

_____

_____

3 Why do you think the job needs people who like being outside?

_____

_____

_____

"I can explain why something happens in a piece of writing."

Section Five — Reading Carefully

Putting Things in Order

You might have to put events in order

Some questions might ask you to put things in order of what happened when.

Mei's Snowman

Mei dashed outside into the fresh, powdery snow. She couldn't wait to get started! **1** First she made two balls of snow and put the smaller one on top of the bigger one. **2** Then she found some sticks to use as arms. **3** She drew on some eyes and a big, smiling mouth and stepped back to admire her work. Something was missing, but Mei had an idea. **4** She took off her woolly hat and placed it on the snowman's head. Now he was perfect.

Look at the text and put these events in order, using the numbers 1 to 4.

Mei gave the snowman sticks for arms.	2
Mei gave the snowman a hat.	4
Mei made two balls of snow.	1
Mei drew a face on the snowman.	3

Section Five — Reading Carefully

Putting Things in Order

Read the pieces of writing below and answer the questions.

> Max steered his boat towards the small beach on the rocky island. As the bottom of the boat scraped on the sand, he jumped out and dragged it out of the water. He set off along the shore, scrambling over rocks and splashing through rock pools, peering around him all the time. As he turned a corner, he saw what he had been looking for — the cave.

1) Put these events in **order**, using the numbers 1 to 4.

Max walked along the shore. ☐   Max sailed to an island. ☐

Max got out of the boat. ☐   Max saw a cave. ☐

> The entrance was blocked by an enormous rock, but Max noticed a gap just big enough for him to squeeze through.
> The ceiling of the cave was so low that Max had to crawl through on his hands and knees. As he moved further into the cave, it grew darker and darker. He fumbled for his torch and switched it on. The light revealed a rusty metal chest, only a metre away. This must be it!

2) Put these events in **order**, using the numbers 1 to 4.

Max turned on a torch. ☐   Max squeezed past a rock. ☐

Max saw a chest. ☐   Max crawled through a cave. ☐

"I can put the events of a text in order."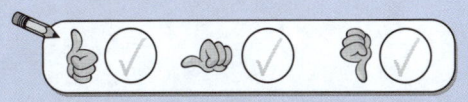

Section Five — Reading Carefully

Thinking About Words

Different words can mean the same thing

Sometimes, you can use more than one word to describe the same thing. The more words you know, the easier it will be to understand a piece of writing.

A Time Travel Adventure

Becky was bored of trudging around the museum. She glanced around her, hoping to see something that would liven up the dreary school trip. In a dark corner, she spotted a small door with a 'Do Not Enter' sign. Becky waited until the teacher had her back turned, then darted through the door.

She found herself in a dimly lit room where gigantic dinosaurs towered over her. They looked surprisingly realistic. Becky closed her eyes as a peculiar feeling came over her.

'peculiar' means 'strange'.

'gigantic' means 'big'.

Find and copy a word from the text which means 'boring'.

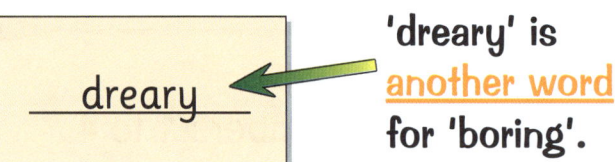

'dreary' is another word for 'boring'.

If you don't know what a word means, use the rest of the sentence to help you.

Section Five — Reading Carefully

Thinking About Words

Answer this question about the story on the previous page.

1 Draw a line to match each word from the text to its meaning.

trudging	moved quickly
darted	walking slowly
realistic	lifelike

Read the next part of the story and answer the questions.

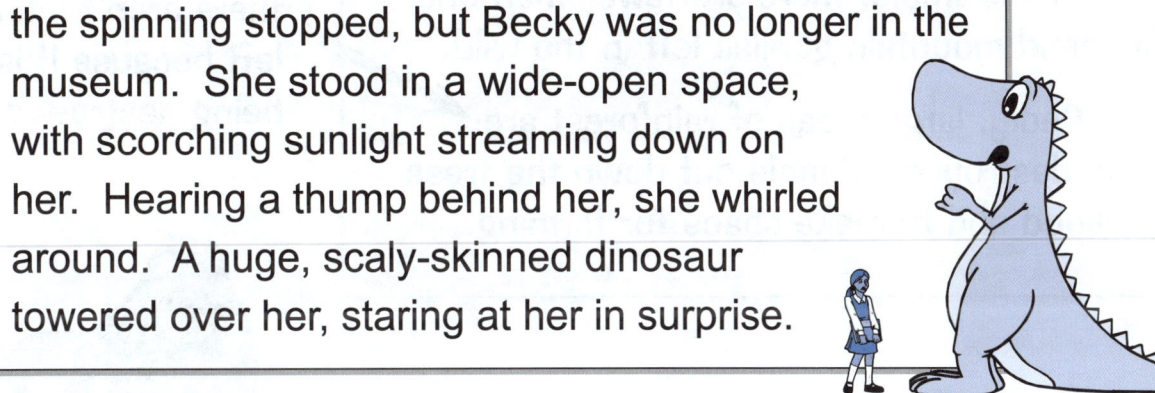

The room began to spin faster and faster. Suddenly, the spinning stopped, but Becky was no longer in the museum. She stood in a wide-open space, with scorching sunlight streaming down on her. Hearing a thump behind her, she whirled around. A huge, scaly-skinned dinosaur towered over her, staring at her in surprise.

2 **Find** and **copy** a word from the text which means 'hot'.

_____

3 What does the word '**whirled**' mean?

_____

"I can find and use different words that mean the same thing."

Section Five — Reading Carefully

Section Six — Thinking About the Text

Making Assumptions

You can guess answers from other details

Sometimes, answers aren't mentioned directly in the text.
But you can make a good guess using other details in the writing.

Rainforests

Rainforests are very important because they are home to nearly half of all the animals and plants in the world. Many animals, including mountain gorillas, tree frogs and macaw parrots, only live in the rainforest. Some of these animals are dying out. For example, there are fewer than one thousand mountain gorillas left in the wild.

Sadly, large areas of rainforest are being destroyed. People cut down the trees for wood and to make space for farming.

Mountain gorillas can only live in the rainforest, so you can assume that there aren't many left because it is being destroyed.

Why aren't there many mountain gorillas left?

The rainforests where they live are being destroyed.

You should say what you think based on what is in the text.

Making Assumptions

Read this piece of writing and answer the questions.

> Rachel stopped at the front door of the spooky house.
>
> "I don't want to go in there," she said. "What if there are spiders?"
>
> "We'll be fine," replied Claire, as she pushed the door. The rusty hinges groaned as it swung open, revealing a gloomy entrance draped with cobwebs.
>
> It was dark in the hallway, and the old wooden furniture was coated in a thick layer of dust.
>
> "I can't wait to explore!" said Claire excitedly, "I've heard that this house is haunted."

1 Who is scared of spiders?

_____

2 Which statement do you think is true? Tick **one** box.

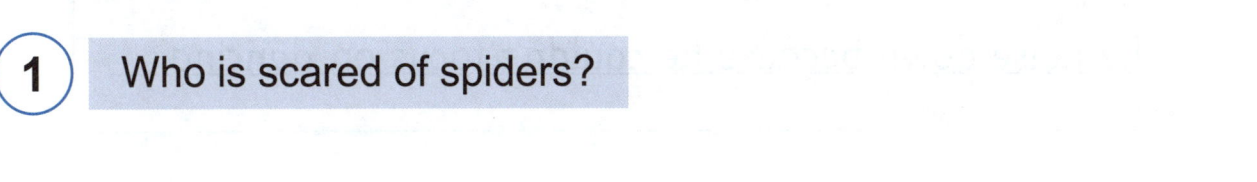

The house has been cleaned recently. ☐

Nobody has lived in the house for a while. ☐

Rachel and Claire go to the house every day. ☐

3 Why do you think Claire wanted to go to the house?

_____

"I can find answers that aren't given directly in a text."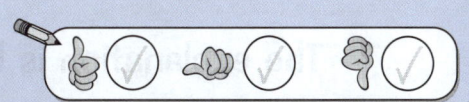

What Happens Next?

Some questions ask what happens next

Some questions ask you to say what happens next. You have to make a guess that is supported by the text — you can't just write anything.

> Dhamesh was practising for his dance show which was just days away. Just as he was mid-spin, a deafening wail of guitars came from next door and Dhamesh stumbled.

What do you think happened next? Why?

> Dhamesh went next door to ask the neighbours to keep the noise down because he couldn't focus on dancing.

You need to explain your answer

You have to explain your choices based on what you've just read.

> The shoemaker was confused. He was sure he'd made eight pairs of shoes, but now there were only seven. Just then, he noticed an elf dashing out of the open door with a shoe in each hand.

What do you think the shoemaker did next? Why?

> He chased the elf because he wanted his shoes back.

The explanation is backed up by the text.

Section Six — Thinking About the Text

What Happens Next?

Read the pieces of writing below and answer the questions.

Roshni had always loved diving and exploring the mysteries of the sea. Today, the water was especially clear, which made the colourful seabed seem even more magical than usual. Roshni was about to swim back to the surface when something gold and shiny caught her eye.

1 What do you think Roshni did next? Why?

_____

_____

Plastic can be very useful, but scientists have recently realised that it's seriously damaging the oceans. For example, when plastic shopping bags are thrown away they can end up in the ocean, where birds and fish may eat them.

2 What do you think people might start doing more now? Why?

_____

_____

"I can guess what happens next based on a piece of writing."

Stories

Stories can be made up or about real events

A story can be about something that actually happened, or something that's made up.

This story is made up:

Maria's Voyage

Maria waited until she could hear her parents snoring in the room next door before she grabbed a lamp and slipped out of the front door. A tear slid down her cheek. She would miss her parents, but she couldn't pass up this chance. The ship sailed at dawn and Maria was determined to be on it.

Over her shoulder she carried a bag of her brother's old clothes. Once she was a safe distance from the house, she would change into them and sneak onto the ship disguised as a cabin boy.

How is Maria planning to get onto the ship?

Use the words from the question to help you find the answer.

She is going to sneak onto the ship disguised as a cabin boy.

Stories

Read the next part of the story and answer the questions.

> Although it was early, the harbour was bustling. Maria hurried to the ship she had chosen, 'The Sea Fairy'. The captain was busy arguing with one of his sailors. While he was distracted, Maria slipped inside a huge wooden box and pulled the lid shut.
>
> After what felt like hours, she felt the ship jerk forwards. Her adventure had begun! Suddenly, the lid of the box opened and she saw the angry face of the captain peering down at her.
>
> "What's this?" he roared. "Looks like we have a stowaway!"

1) What does '**bustling**' mean? Tick **one** box.

quiet ☐   busy ☐   scary ☐   dirty ☐

2) Put these events in **order**, using the numbers 1 to 3.

The captain discovered Maria. ☐

Maria hid in a box. ☐

The captain argued with a sailor. ☐

3) What do you think happens next? **Why?**

_____

_____

"I can answer questions about stories."

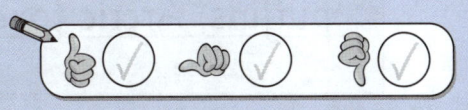

Section Seven — Types of Text

Information Texts

Information texts are usually full of facts

You might be asked to find facts in information texts.
This information text contains lots of facts about Iceland.

Iceland

Iceland is an island just south of the Arctic Circle.

Why Do People Visit Iceland?

Lots of people visit Iceland all year round to swim in the hot springs, which are pools of water heated by the earth. Many visitors come in the summer because the days are so long that you can see the sun at midnight. In winter, you can explore ice caves (caves formed in ice by water running through it).

What Lives in Iceland?

Despite its name, some parts of Iceland are very green, with lots of plants. Iceland is also home to lots of animals. On the coast you can see puffins, and inland there are Arctic foxes and Icelandic horses.

Read the text carefully to find the fact you need.

Give three animals that you can see in Iceland.

puffins, Arctic foxes and Icelandic horses

Information Texts

Answer this question about the piece of writing on the previous page.

1 Which of these can you **not** see in Iceland in summer? Tick **one** box.

hot springs ☐   the midnight sun ☐   ice caves ☐

Read the next part of the text and answer the questions.

> **People in Iceland**
> The first people to visit Iceland were Irish monks, who arrived over a thousand years ago. However, the earliest people to settle there were the Vikings, who arrived a hundred years later.
>
> Today, most people in Iceland live in the capital city, Reykjavik. Other parts of the country are difficult to live in because of the cold weather and mountainous landscape.

2 Which **two** groups of people are mentioned as coming to Iceland?

_____

3 Why do most people in Iceland live in Reykjavik?

_____

_____

"I can answer questions about information texts."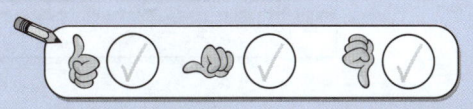

Section Seven — Types of Text

Poems

Poems are different to stories

Poems are pieces of writing that are often written in short lines and have lots of description.

Don't be put off by a poem — read it carefully and you can find the answer.

The Astronaut

If I could float above the Earth
And see the seas so blue,
If I could see the land so green,
I know what I would do.

I'd take a picture in my mind
So I would not forget
How special our home planet is,
Each rainbow and sunset.

When I got back to solid ground,
I'd shout out on the spot:
"Protect the Earth — it is our home,
The only one we've got."

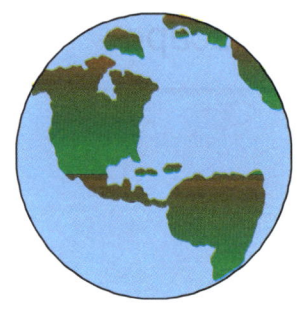

What does the person in the poem imagine they are doing?

Floating in the air and looking down on the Earth.

Section Seven — Types of Text

Poems

Answer this question about the poem on the previous page.

1) Why does the writer say we need to protect the Earth?

_____

Read this poem and answer the questions.

The Forest Fairies
The forest fairies hide
Whenever someone's near.
And though they can't be seen,
I know they're always here.

The oak tree is their home,
And I have heard it told
That when the summer fades,
They turn the leaves to gold.

2) Why can't the forest fairies be seen?

_____

3) What time of year do the fairies turn the leaves gold?

_____

"I can answer questions about poems."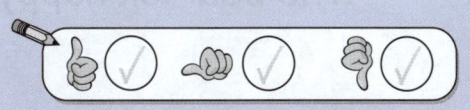

Section Seven — Types of Text

Year Two Objectives Test

1 The sentence below is missing a **capital letter**.
Tick **one** box to show where the capital letter should go.

Amaru **is** going on a **t**rip to **g**lasgow.

1 mark

2 Add '**s**' or '**es**' to the words below to make them **plural**.

match_____   chicken_____   grass_____

1 mark

3 What type of word is underlined in the sentence below? Tick **one** box.

Suyin <u>bravely</u> jumped into the water.

a noun ☐   an adjective ☐

a verb ☐   an adverb ☐

1 mark

4 Complete each sentence with the correct **punctuation mark**.

How did you do that __

Tom enjoys football __ dancing and music.

The bear felt happy after a long sleep __

1 mark

5 Draw a line to match each sentence to the correct **sentence type**.

I don't like parrots.   question

Where are you going?   statement

What big teeth you have!   exclamation

1 mark

6 Circle the **correct** spelling in each pair of words.

chork / chalk   germ / jerm   squirrel / squirral

1 mark

7 Complete each word with '**tion**' or '**sion**'.

erup_____   explo_____   opera_____

1 mark

8 Complete each sentence using the **joining words** in the boxes. Use each joining word **once**.

because   when   but

I'll see you _____ you get home.

Mumbi wore a coat _____ it was raining.

She likes apples, _____ she hates oranges.

1 mark

Year Two Objectives Test

Read the story and answer the questions below.

> The rabbit and the elephant lived next door to each other. Every morning, the rabbit went to his field to grow vegetables. As he passed by the elephant's house, he asked her to join him. They walked to the fields together and chatted about vegetables. They enjoyed spending time together. The elephant grew peas and beans, and the rabbit grew pumpkins.

9 **How often** did the rabbit go to his field? Tick **one** box.

every week ☐   never ☐

every other day ☐   every day ☐

1 mark

10 Write down the **two** things that the elephant grew in her field.

_____

_____

1 mark

11 How do you know that the rabbit and the elephant are **friends**?

_____

1 mark

Year Two Objectives Test

Read the text and answer the questions below.

> **Shipwreck Rescue**
>
> Grace Darling was born in the north-east of England in 1815. Her father was a lighthouse keeper. One day, Grace spotted a ship that had crashed into some rocks. Grace and her father rowed a small boat across the sea to rescue the sailors. The sea was rough and Grace was frightened.

12 What **job** did Grace's father have?

_____

1 mark

13 **Why** did the sailors need rescuing?

_____

_____

1 mark

14 How do you know that the weather was **stormy**?

_____

1 mark

15 Find and copy a word from the text that means '**scared**'.

_____

1 mark

Year Two Objectives Test

Glossary

Adjective	A word that describes a noun, e.g. yellow gloves.
Adverb	A word that describes a verb, e.g. I ran quickly.
Apostrophe '	Used to show missing letters and that something belongs to someone, e.g. can't, Mo's violin.
Capital letter	Used at the start of sentences as well as for names of people, places, days of the week, months of the year and for 'I', e.g. Tom, Friday.
Comma ,	Used to separate items in a list, e.g. I like apples, bananas and peaches.
Command	A sentence which gives orders, e.g. Go home now.
Compound word	A word that's made up of two other words, e.g. toothbrush = tooth + brush.
Consonant	Every letter of the alphabet except 'a', 'e', 'i', 'o' and 'u'.
Exclamation	A sentence which shows strong feelings. They start with 'what' or 'how', e.g. How angry I am!
Exclamation mark !	Used at the end of sentences showing strong feelings and for some commands, e.g. I'm scared of snakes!
Full stop .	Used to show the end of a sentence, e.g. I love dogs.
Homophone	A word that sounds the same as another word but is spelt differently and means something else, e.g. been and bean.

Glossary

Joining word	A word which joins other words or sentences together, e.g. 'and' — fish and chips.
Noun	A name for objects, places and people, e.g. medal.
Noun phrase	A group of words including a noun which give more information about the noun, e.g. this bag, a hot day.
Plural	More than one of something, e.g. cups.
Question	A sentence which asks something, e.g. Where are we going?
Question mark ?	Used at the end of questions.
Silent letter	A letter that you don't say when reading a word aloud, e.g. two.
Simple past	The tense used to talk about things in the past.
Simple present	The tense used to talk about what's happening now.
Singular	One of something, e.g. pencil.
Statement	A sentence which tells you something, e.g. I'm sad.
Suffix	A letter or letters that are added to the end of a word to make a new word, e.g. playful.
Verb	A doing or being word, e.g. eat, speak, am.
Vowel	The letters 'a', 'e', 'i', 'o' and 'u'.

Answers

Start of Year Two Test

Q1 You should have circled: **amy, tuesday, july**
(1 mark for all 3 correct)

Q2 boot — flute
fern — burn
snail — pale
(1 mark for all 3 correct)

Q3 **thank**
(1 mark)

Q4 What is your name — **?**
What fun this is — **!**
I like strawberries — **.**
(1 mark for all 3 correct)

Q5 Steve plays the guitar.
(1 mark)

Q6 **c**rab, **f**ly, **s**wim, **t**rain
(1 mark for all 4 correct)

Q7 You should have ticked:
The cow eats the grass.
Rumi is my best friend.
(1 mark for both correct)

Q8 **beard, toilet, night**
(1 mark for all 3 correct)

Q9 You should have ticked:
Katya is playing basketball.
Ekrem throws the ball.
Dan and Jo are skating.
(1 mark for all 3 correct)

Q10 A card / A yellow card with flowers on it.
(1 mark)

Q11 You should have ticked: **happy**
(1 mark)

Q12 You should have ticked: **a bouncy castle**
(1 mark)

Q13 At three o'clock.
(1 mark)

Q14 You should have ticked: **Tommy's present**
(1 mark)

Q15 Any sensible answer, for example:
It is the best present.
(1 mark)

Section One — Grammar

Page 7 — Nouns and Noun Phrases

Q1 I dropped the **ball**.
Eric is my best friend.
We are going to **Spain**.

Q2 You should have circled: **bike, fireworks, chickens**

Q3 You should have ticked: **the red door, that book, a giant shoe**

Page 9 — Verbs

Q1 You should have ticked: **sing, speak, begin**

Q2 Esmee **walks** her pet dog.
My sister and I **love** watching TV.
The cat **sleeps** by the fire.

Q3

Verb	Verb + 'ing'
float	floating
laugh	**laughing**
roll	**rolling**
stamp	**stamping**

Page 11 — Adjectives

Q1 I saw a **cheeky** monkey at the zoo.
There is **melted** chocolate on the sofa!
The bees were **busy** making honey.

Q2 You should have circled: the **fancy** hat, the **hot** weather, the book was **old**

Q3 My sister is tall**er** than me.
I can jump the high**est** in my class.
Arlo's bedroom is clean**er** than Erin's.

Page 13 — Adverbs

Q1 You should have ticked:
Yuri speaks **politely**.
Kat **correctly** guessed the answer.

Q2 He **carefully** poured the water.
The music was playing **noisily**.

Q3

adjective	adverb
mad	**madly**
fair	**fairly**
sleepy	**sleepily**
healthy	**healthily**

Answers

Page 15 — Types of Sentences

Q1 The lemon is sour. — **statement**
How old are you? — **question**
Kelly plays football. — **statement**
Where is the bus? — **question**
What time is it? — **question**
I lost my shoe. — **statement**

Q2 You should have ticked:
What a hard race that was!
How nice to see you again!

Q3 Put that book away. — **command**
Why did you do that? — **question**
How lovely that was! — **exclamation**
Bananas are yellow. — **statement**

Page 17 — Tenses

Q1 You should have circled: **we landed, I finished, Priya jumped**

Q2

simple present	simple past
I live	**I lived**
Zoe packs	Zoe packed
Ben washes	**Ben washed**

Q3 Sam **uses** glasses when she reads.
Mum watched as I **stirred** the soup.
She **asked** before she played outside.

Page 19 — Joining Words

Q1 We can have lunch **if** you are hungry.
Lucy saw Libby **when** she was shopping.
Jamal wore a hat **that** his mum knitted.

Q2 I got in trouble **because** of my sister.
Simon liked the picture **that** I drew.
They went to bed, **but** they weren't tired.
Dad cooked dinner **and** it was tasty.

Q3 I got new shoes, **but** they were too small.
His sister is five **and** his brother is six.
Put your coat on **or** you will get cold.

Section Two — Punctuation

Page 21 — Capital Letters

Q1 **Eli** uses capital letters correctly.

Q2 mountain — **no capital letter**
water — **no capital letter**
emily — **capital letter**
england — **capital letter**
bottle — **no capital letter**
monday — **capital letter**

Q3 Next week, **I** am going to **F**rance.
Let's visit **M**ike on **S**unday.

Page 23 — Ending Sentences

Q1 You should have ticked:
I am going to the shop
I'll be back soon

Q2 You should have ticked:
Can you get me a drink?
Is this your hat?

Q3 What a **big hill that is!**

Page 25 — Commas

Q1 You should have ticked:
The water was deep, dark and cold.
I saw fish, crabs and a shark.

Q2 Lara is scared of spiders**,** wasps and lions.
My brothers are called Ed**,** Ted and Ned.
You can play football**,** hockey or cricket.

Q3 I drink juice, water and milk.
Violet doesn't like maths, art or music.

Page 27 — Apostrophes

Q1 I **haven't** got a coat.
I know **he's** hiding somewhere.
They **won't** eat cabbage.

Q2 I like my teacher because **she's** kind.
My dad **can't** find his tie.
The sun **hasn't** come out yet.

Q3 It's **Kit's** book.
It's **Raj's** puppy.
It's **Liz's** pen.

Section Three — Vocabulary

Page 29 — Suffixes — Plurals

Q1 house**s**
lion**s**
sash**es**
gas**es**
beach**es**
nose**s**

Q2 stor**ies**
pen**nies**
bod**ies**
valley**s**
holiday**s**
famil**ies**

Answers

Q3 You should have ticked:
I want to travel to other **countries**.
I have two **bunches** of bananas.

Page 31 — Suffixes — Other Endings

Q1 You should have shaded in **less** and **ful**.

Q2 The monkey is very **cheerful**.
I was shocked at his **rudeness**.
Their **punishment** was fair.
Indu was totally **speechless**.

Q3 You should have ticked:
He was always very careful.

The correct suffixes are:
useness — **ful**
darkment — **ness**

Page 33 — Compound Words

Q1 You should have circled: **hairbrush, suitcase, bathroom**

Q2 shoe — lace
pan — **cake**
eye — **brow**
grand — **son**

Q3 For example, you could have added:
foot + **ball** = **football**
book + **shelf** = **bookshelf**
snow + **man** = **snowman**

Section Four — Spelling

Page 35 — Vowel Sounds

Q1 You should have circled:
pain, play, stray, fake, blame, stain

Q2 The mouse ate all of our ch**ee**se.
The pr**ie**st said a prayer.
The queen held a f**ea**st.

Q3 w**a**nder, forg**o**t, **o**range, sw**a**llow

Q4 The sky looked dark and grey.
Sati is very pol**i**te.
The butterfly has br**igh**t wings.

Page 37 — Vowel Sounds

Q1 You should have ticked:
fall, yawn, warm

Q2 We hid under the **covers**.
The **drummer** played us a beat.
The **monkey** swings in the trees.

Q3 w___ld — or (**world**)
c___ve — ur (**curve**)
tw___rl — ir (**twirl**)
p___son — er (**person**)

Page 39 — The Soft 'c' and Hard 'c' Sounds

Q1 You should have circled:
sort, salad, dancing, celebrate

Q2 We need a map and a **c**ompass.
Maria played a song on the **k**eyboard.
The elephant was stu**ck**.

Q3 celery — soft 'c'
carrot — hard 'c'
surfer — soft 'c'
octagon — hard 'c'

Page 41 — The Soft 'g' Sound

Q1 You should have circled:
ledge, fridge, age, badge, image, manage

Q2 The guide says we will need lots of ener**g**y, so we should take sugary snacks. I baked some **g**in**g**er biscuits and an**g**el cakes.

Q3 Don't stand too close to the **e**d**g**e.
The warrior had coura**g**e.
The car en**g**ine is broken.
Marcus is good at **j**uggling.

Page 43 — Silent 'k', 'g' and 'w'

Q1 **k**nife, **w**riggle, **w**rap, **k**nuckle, **g**nat, **g**narled

Q2 silent 'k' — knee, knot
silent 'g' — gnarl
silent 'w' — wrestle, writer
no silent letter — kangaroo, goat

Q3 The dog **knawed** the bone. — g
We **gnocked** on the door. — k
Amir broke his **rrist**. — w
I **gnew** we had the wrong answer. — k

Page 45 — Words Ending in 'le', 'el', 'al' and 'il'

Q1 You should have ticked:
petal, gerbil, table

Q2 In Apr**il**, I am going to trav**el** to Wales with my family. We have to fit all of our things in our litt**le** car. While we are away, I want to try some loc**al** food.

Q3 There are scary creatures in the jung**le**.
We dug a secret tunn**el** in our garden.

Answers

My favourite animal is a sloth.
The witch cast an evil spell.

Page 47 — The 'zh' Sound and Words Ending in 'tion'

Q1 You should have circled:
leisure, unusual, decision

Q2 There was an **explosion** in the lab.
Laura loves **action** films.
The **television** was too loud.
The magic **potion** turns you into a frog.

Q3 I wear glasses because my vi___ is poor. — sion
Walk with cau___ on the ice. — tion
In my confu___, I forgot my wallet. — sion
I asked for a bigger por___. — tion

Page 49 — Adding 'ing', 'ed', 'er', 'est' & 'y' to Words

Q1 Andrew **loved** travelling by train.
I'm **moving** house next month.
May **baked** a cake, and she ate it all.

Q2 Rachel carr**ied** the dog across the river.
I spent all day tid**y**ing my room.
Rob destro**yed** his sandcastle.
The snails hurr**ied** as fast as they could.

Q3

	ing	ed
live	living	lived
annoy	annoying	annoyed
fry	frying	fried
dive	diving	dived

Page 51 — Adding 'ing', 'ed', 'er', 'est' & 'y' to Words

Q1 You should have circled:
pop, rob, drag

Q2 The rhino is nap**ping** in the sun.
I am listen**ing** to music.
Sobia is cut**ting** the grass.

Q3

	er	est
long	longer	longest
strange	stranger	strangest
comfy	comfier	comfiest

Q4 **handy, snappy, icy**

Page 53 — Homophones and Other Words

Q1 I can **hear** music coming from upstairs.
The **bee** is buzzing from flower to flower.
Alex is going **to** the cinema.
We are going in **their** car.

Q2 Mum won't let me clim**b** the tree.
There is a pot of g**o**ld at the end of the rainbow.
We are two **h**ours away from the airport.
I packed some cl**ot**hes for my holiday.

Q3 There is a monster behined the sofa. — **behind**
The artwork in the school is pritty. — **pretty**
The beach is very bisy today. — **busy**

Section Five — Reading Carefully

Page 55 — Finding Information — Stories

Q1 You should have ticked:
getting lost in the forest

Q2 **a map, a compass**

Q3 He plodded away. / He walked away.

Page 57 — Finding Information — Non-fiction

Q1 You should have ticked:
What to feed your gecko
Where to keep your gecko

Q2 every two days

Q3 a heat lamp

Page 59 — Explaining Why

Q1 You should have ticked:
The writer only wants people who are free in July to apply.

Q2 There are more dogs to look after because lots of people are going on holiday.

Q3 The job involves taking dogs for walks, so people need to enjoy being outside.

Page 61 — Putting Things in Order

Q1 Max walked along the shore. — 3
Max got out of the boat. — 2
Max sailed to an island. — 1
Max saw a cave. — 4

Answers

Q2 Max turned on a torch. — 3
Max saw a chest. — 4
Max squeezed past a rock. — 1
Max crawled through a cave. — 2

Page 63 — Thinking About Words

Q1 trudging — walking slowly
darted — moved quickly
realistic — lifelike

Q2 scorching

Q3 Any suitable answer, for example: turned around quickly

Section Six — Thinking About the Text

Page 65 — Making Assumptions

Q1 Rachel

Q2 You should have ticked:
Nobody has lived in the house for a while.

Q3 Any suitable answer, for example: She wanted to see a ghost.

Page 67 — What Happens Next?

Q1 Any suitable answer, for example: She dives down because she wants to see the gold object.

Q2 Any suitable answer, for example: They might start reusing bags instead of throwing them away, so they don't end up in the ocean.

Section Seven — Types of Text

Page 69 — Stories

Q1 You should have ticked: **busy**

Q2 The captain discovered Maria. — 3
Maria hid in a box. — 2
The captain argued with a sailor. — 1

Q3 Any suitable answer, for example: The captain is cross with Maria, but lets her stay on the ship because it's too late to take her back.

Page 71 — Information Texts

Q1 You should have ticked:
ice caves

Q2 Irish monks and Vikings

Q3 Any suitable answer, for example:
The weather and landscape make it hard to live in other parts of the country.

Page 73 — Poems

Q1 It's the only planet we have.

Q2 Any suitable answer, for example: They hide when people are near.

Q3 Autumn / The end of summer

Year Two Objectives Test

Q1 You should have ticked: **glasgow**
(1 mark)

Q2 match**es**, chicken**s**, grass**es**
(1 mark for all 3 correct)

Q3 You should have ticked: **an adverb**
(1 mark)

Q4 How did you do that**?**
Tom enjoys football**,** dancing and music.
The bear felt happy after a long sleep**.**
(1 mark for all 3 correct)

Q5 I don't like parrots. — statement
Where are you going? — question
What big teeth you have! — exclamation
(1 mark for all 3 correct)

Q6 You should have circled: **chalk**, **germ**, **squirrel**
(1 mark for all 3 correct)

Q7 erup**tion**, explo**sion**, opera**tion**
(1 mark for all 3 correct)

Q8 I'll see you **when** you get home.
Mumbi wore a coat **because** it was raining.
She likes apples, **but** she hates oranges.
(1 mark for all 3 correct)

Q9 You should have ticked: **every day**
(1 mark)

Q10 peas and beans
(1 mark for both correct)

Q11 Any sensible answer, for example:
They enjoyed spending time together.
(1 mark)

Q12 lighthouse keeper
(1 mark)

Q13 Their ship had crashed into some rocks.
(1 mark)

Q14 The sea was rough.
(1 mark)

Q15 frightened
(1 mark)